The Feelings Activity Book for Toddlers

The Feelings Activity Book
FOR TODDLERS

50 Fun Activities to Identify, Understand, and Manage Big Feelings

STACY SPENSLEY

ROCKRIDGE PRESS

For all the parents out there just
trying to do your best. You've got this.

First Rockridge Press trade paperback edition 2022

Rockridge Press and the Rockridge Press logo are trademarks or registered trademarks of Callisto Media Inc. and/or its affiliates in the United States and other countries and may not be used without written permission.

For general information on our other products and services, please contact our Customer Care Department within the United States at (866) 744-2665, or outside the United States at (510) 253-0500.

Paperback ISBN: 978-1-68539-894-1 | eBook ISBN: 979-8-88608-128-2

Manufactured in the United States of America

Interior and Cover Designer: Brieanna Felschow
Art Producer: Maya Melenchuk
Editor: Sasha Henriques
Production Editor: Jaime Chan
Production Manager: Riley Hoffman

All illustrations used under license from Shutterstock.com

10 9 8 7 6 5 4 3 2 1 0

CONTENTS

- 1 -
How to Introduce Feelings

The toddler years can be some of the most fun and the most fraught. Once babies have mastered some gross motor skills and are mobile, their curious brains start building millions of synaptic connections every minute. All this brain growth supports their social and emotional development—they now have opinions, feelings, wants, and likes beyond the immediate needs of infancy.

If you, like many parents, were raised to suppress emotions and discouraged from discussing them, toddlerhood can be stressful. It also makes this age the perfect time to build a strong foundation for your child to talk about and process emotions. The activities in this book are meant to help you connect with your little one, support their emotional development, and give them the vocabulary to help manage their feelings as they grow.

Children learn best through play, so the emotional learning is really a side benefit to having fun together. Building that connection with your child is the foundation of them feeling safe.

Toddlers Have Feelings

When I was a first-time parent, the toddler stage often felt like a mini version of *Survivor: Emotions*. Now I'm wrapping up my third toddler rodeo and I have a lot more skills and strategies than I did during the first two rounds. After almost a decade as a parenting coach (and a mother), I've supported hundreds of families through the transition to toddlerhood. The methods that worked to meet the needs of your baby don't work the same with a mobile, opinionated toddler, and it can be exhausting.

Instead of trying to soothe a toddler or "fix" their feelings, hold space for them to work it out safely. The world is a big, new place, and intense feelings can be overwhelming—for both of you. As parents we must model how to manage emotions and support our children through them. Using the activities in this book can offer a shared vocabulary and strategies to help you through.

Understanding Emotion

Emotions are the physiological responses your body has to stimuli; feelings are the ways you cognitively process and describe those emotions. Toddlers make huge developmental leaps in their communication skills, so a big part of supporting their emotional intelligence is helping them interpret those physical reactions so they can identify them.

During big emotional reactions, the brain goes into fight-flight-or-freeze mode and literally shuts down other parts of the brain for pure survival. When someone, an adult or a child, is upset, you cannot reason with them. Applying logic when a toddler is upset isn't possible, though it's tempting to "correct" big feelings in the moment. But emotions are neither good nor bad—they're part of the human experience.

The best time to talk about feelings is when no one is upset. The hard part is remembering to talk about them when the situation isn't urgent, but that's one way these activities can help. It's also important for children to know that adults also have big feelings and use a variety of strategies to stay calm. Normalizing having those feelings, naming them, and learning how to manage them are powerful skills to practice.

Benefits of Learning through Play

Children are like sponges: They're learning all the time, and most effectively through play. Their receptive language skills are growing by leaps and bounds at this stage, but they also require a lot of repetition (yes, that's why they bring you the same book 11 zillion times). It's easy to assume that once you've told a toddler something they will remember it, but it's unfortunately not true. Also, knowing something and being able to implement it in the moment when you're upset is still challenging for adults with decades of life experience.

Playing with purpose gives children the chance to practice and develop new skills repeatedly in a physically and emotionally safe environment. It lets them practice social interactions, turn-taking, listening, fine and gross motor skills, and more.

Toddler Time

Toddlers have short attention spans—really short. The activities in this book shouldn't take long to set up, because they aren't going to last long, and that's totally normal. The activities relate to various developmental skills, but every child is different. Not everything they do needs to be challenging, and during periods of growth it can be helpful for kids to practice skills they've mastered to improve their confidence. The point is to have fun, and no one is having fun (or learning) if they're frustrated.

Even though developmental milestones are simply signposts along the way, each activity lists specific skills that relate to that particular activity. If you want to focus on particular areas, you can choose activities based on the skills listed. Or just choose something that sounds enjoyable and consider the skill practice a side benefit.

Gross motor activities (large body movements) can help regulate emotions and provide an outlet for anger and frustration. Improving fine motor skills can help communication and independence, which reduces misunderstandings. Language skills, which are receptive and expressive, are not all verbal or spoken. And all that improves communication, which allows better social interactions.

Toddlers have limited power and control over their lives. They want to be more independent, but they also want to stay safe. Playing with them so they have more opportunities to make choices and communicate can make everyone's life easier.

Skills Learned

Each activity notes skills from the following list that apply to that exercise. Every child develops at their own pace, so some activities will be easier or harder than others based on your child's current skills. If your child struggles with some activities, especially at first, that's to be expected.

cognitive skills

receptive communication

expressive communication

sensory skills

fine motor skills

social skills

gross motor skills

Safety First!

My second child's first word was (not kidding) "daredevil," and my third's nickname is Danger Baby. The activities in this book are all aimed at kids who are too young to be alone, but some of them require closer supervision than others. You know your child best—some kids put everything in their mouths while others don't, some look before they leap, etc.

Some activities will include a caution note in case of safety risks. Again, precautions you take will depend on your child's personality, skills, and age, but it's better to be on the safe side. Since toddlers can't read, they'll need help with setup anyway, but there will be a note if cutting with a knife or scissors is required, if small objects are a choking hazard, or if other possible safety precautions are needed.

How to Use This Book

There's a big difference between a 12-month-old and a 36-month-old, but they're both considered toddlers. This book covers the entire age range, although most toddlers' attention spans and physical skills will improve as they get older. Each activity is meant to help facilitate discussion about emotions and feelings so your child can build their emotional vocabulary and develop strategies for age-appropriate co-regulation (using your own warm, empathetic presence to help your child calm their own nervous system).

The 50 activities take 5 to 30 minutes each and are divided into four chapters: How I Feel, How My Body Feels, Feelings about Others, and What to Do When I Have Big Feelings. You can read through in order, flip through at random, or look for specific skills or emotions. It's okay to move on to other activities if an activity is outside your toddler's capabilities. The materials called for are inexpensive and easily accessible, and the ones you'll need are listed for each activity. Getting messy can be inevitable with toddlers, but the estimated mess potential is noted on each page using a scale of 1 (no mess) to 5 (sorry).

Not every activity will work for every child, but variations and adaptations to meet a variety of needs and situations are included whenever possible.

- 2 -
How I Feel

In this chapter, you'll find activities that help toddlers explore and identify different types of feelings. Naming feelings and learning how they are expressed creates a shared vocabulary to improve communication. There are some arts and crafts, games, and simple activities to share with your little one.

1. Thumbs-Up/Thumbs-Down

This is a simple game to teach toddlers how to express opinions, practice empathy, and work on both receptive and expressive communication skills. You can adjust the questions and possible responses as your child gains new skills.

Messiness: 1

Activity Time: 5 to 10 minutes

STEPS:

1. For the youngest toddlers, ask if they like something and have them reply "yes" or "no" by nodding, pointing, or replying verbally.

2. For older toddlers, ask if they like something and have them give a thumbs-up or thumbs-down to indicate their choice.

3. Mix up simple examples with situations like "Does going to the park make you angry? Happy? Sad?"

   TIP: *With no prep or supplies required, this is an easy game to play in the car or to pass the time while waiting in line.*

2. Paper Plate Faces

Making these crafty faces is a fun art activity and gives toddlers a chance to consider what makes a face express a certain feeling. Once the art portion is complete, you can use the plate faces to help your toddler identify and name those feelings. You can even use them as masks or puppets later. The listed materials are starting points, but feel free to get creative with what you have.

Messiness: 2 (unless you add more materials)

Activity Time: 20 minutes

MATERIALS:

- ☐ 5 paper plates
- ☐ Crayons or markers
- ☐ White glue or craft glue
- ☐ Wooden craft sticks

STEPS:

1. On each paper plate, draw a face to represent a feeling. You can start with happy, sad, mad, surprised, and scared.

2. Pick an emotion. Have your toddler choose a color to reflect that emotion and color the face.

3. After the coloring and drawing are complete, use the glue to attach a craft stick to the back of each plate. Let the glue dry before using the plate face.

4. Point to each face and name the feeling. Or, you can name the feeling and ask your toddler to point to or hold up the right face. If your toddler can speak, you can have them say the answer.

5. For older toddlers, give them an example situation and ask how they would feel, then have them point to or hold up the face that reflects that feeling. For example: "If you had a new toy that broke, how would you feel? Happy or sad?"

TIP: *Stack the plates to conveniently store them.*

SKILLS
LEARNED

expressive
communication

receptive
communication

3. Morning Affirmations

Emotions are physiological reactions to stimuli, and sometimes simply waking up is enough to cause big feelings. Before you even get out of bed, you can say affirmations to create a positive experience before the transition to facing the world. Affirmations are positive phrases that set an intention and mood for the day. A few minutes of connection with your toddler can help start the morning off with less stress, which can help your child manage their feelings better throughout the day.

Messiness: 1

Preparation Time:
5 minutes

Activity Time: 5 minutes

PREPARATION:

Choose or create an affirmation. Here are some ideas.

▸ I am happy.

▸ I am loved.

▸ I am learning.

▸ I am safe.

▸ Mistakes are ok.

▸ I am doing my best.

STEPS:

1. In the morning, pick an affirmation or two to say. This could be before your toddler gets out of bed, before breakfast, or while you're all in the car.

2. For younger or nonspeaking toddlers, say it for them. Older toddlers can repeat after you or choose one for themselves. This is also a wonderful opportunity to introduce your toddler to ASL if they are nonspeaking.

4. Three Things

Toddlers don't understand abstract concepts like gratitude and time, but that doesn't preclude them from learning about such concepts early. Studies have shown psychological benefits to having a gratitude practice, and people with a higher base level of gratitude tend to be happier. When kids have strong feelings, they believe they will feel that way forever. Thinking about and acknowledging the positive aspects of their lives can help make those parts of the day more concrete.

Messiness: 1

Activity Time: 5 minutes

STEPS:

1. Name three things out loud that you are grateful for today. Start with people you know or tangible things that younger kids can easily understand.

2. For younger or nonspeaking toddlers, you can guess what they might be grateful for and ask them to confirm.

   TIP: *If you can make an audio or video recording of this, it can be a very sweet clip to share when your child is older.*

SKILLS
LEARNED

cognitive
skills

fine motor
skills

social
skills

5. Draw Your Day

This can be a daily practice in the middle or at the end of the day, or it can be something you do with your toddler when they could use some help processing the emotions they've experienced. This activity helps little ones think about their day and connect various events to feelings. This type of discussion helps build the foundation for collaborative problem-solving when they're older.

Messiness: 1

Activity Time: 10 minutes

MATERIALS:

☐ Paper (or a notebook to create a sort of journal)

☐ Pen, pencil, or writing utensil of choice

STEPS:

1. Write the day and date at the top of a piece of paper. Work with your child to recall and write down the activities you've done that day. Since toddlers are still new to navigating the world, small, obvious details are actually very helpful for them. For example: you woke up, got out of bed, ate breakfast, and got dressed. Then you walked to the park to play on the swings, stopped at the grocery store, ate lunch, and then took a nap.

2. Draw a simple picture to go with each activity. The picture for "wake up" could be a sun rising, a bed, or an alarm clock. "Breakfast" could be a piece of toast or a sunny-side up egg, even if they ate something different.

3. Depending on their ability, describe or ask your child how they felt about each activity on the list. Were they excited? Bored? Tired? Write that down, too. Add a drawing of a face that shows that feeling. "When you got dressed you were frustrated, because you wanted to do it by yourself and you needed some help."

4. This is a great activity for around midday to reflect on the morning, and because it's early enough that they're not too tired. Do this as a regular practice to see how your child's memory, observations, and awareness change over time.

5. Let your child add art or color. You might suggest they choose a color to express how they felt about an activity, or they can suggest details to add to your drawings.

   TIP: *Let your child help with the art.*

6. Mountains and Valleys

Young children's feelings may be intense, but they're usually short-lived. Their worldview is still small, so their toy is as important to them as a car or a house to an adult. This exercise helps kids practice putting the highs and lows of the day in perspective, since there are happy moments and challenges mixed throughout. Right now, the whole day may feel like a valley, but it's not a valley without mountains.

Messiness: 1

Activity Time: 10 minutes

STEPS:

1. Ask everyone to take turns and name something that made them happy today (their mountain) and something that was frustrating or hard (their valley).

2. Empathize with their frustration, and when possible, suggest a way to make that situation easier in the future.

TIP: *This is a great activity to do around the dinner table and reflect on the day.*

7. Thumbprint Faces

This classic childhood art project may not seem educational, but along with the fine motor practice, you can use it to build your child's emotional vocabulary by teaching your child how to recognize different emotions on each thumbprint face you create. Toddlers need a lot of repetition as they strengthen all those new neural connections, so having multiple ways to show what feelings look like and what they're called helps the information stick.

Messiness: 3
(if they escape without washing their hands)

Preparation Time:
5 minutes

Activity Time: 10 minutes

MATERIALS:

☐ Paper

☐ Ink pad or washable paint

☐ Pen

PREPARATION:

▹ You may want to cover your work surface for easy cleanup.

▹ Having a wet washcloth on standby is easier than chasing down a kid with ink on their hands!

STEPS:

1. Carefully help your child press their thumb onto the ink pad. Press their thumb on the paper to leave a print.

2. Add some of your own fingerprints for bigger ovals.

3. Use the pen to draw faces on the thumbs. Have your child play "art director," or let them be creative.

SKILLS
LEARNED

gross motor
skills

receptive
communication

sensory
skills

8. Mad Monster

Anger is often mislabeled as a "bad" emotion, but it's a reasonable reaction in many situations. This activity lets your child accept anger as a normal emotional response but also helps them learn to channel the feeling appropriately.

Messiness: 1

Activity Time: 5 minutes

STEPS:

1. When your child is calm, ask them how they would act if they were an angry monster. Would they stomp their feet? Have claws? What would their face look like?

2. Encourage them to hit a pillow or cushion or throw something soft. The physical impact can have a regulating effect on the body, and using a soft object minimizes the potential for injury.

3. Be your own Mad Monster to show them that grown-ups have feelings, too!

9. Soapy Smiles

Emotions are physical sensations, so when your child's body is overstimulated, uncomfortable, or in pain, it's more difficult for them to manage their feelings. The smooth sensation of shaving cream as a craft medium helps soothe the nervous system, and the cleanup couldn't be easier.

Messiness: 4

Activity Time: 10 minutes

MATERIALS:

☐ Unscented shaving cream

STEPS:

1. In a shower or bathtub, spray a quarter-size glob of shaving cream on the tile.

2. Let your little one foam up the shaving cream. Model using a finger to draw a smiley face in the foam, and verbally label it as happy. Let your child copy the smiley face you draw. Model drawing a frowny face, label it as sad, and let your child copy it. Continue modeling and labeling as long as they enjoy the activity, spraying more shaving cream as needed.

3. Rinse it all off before they get out of the bath.

CAUTION: *Never leave a child unattended near water.*

10. What Would You Do?

Toddlers are only starting to understand the very basics of empathy around age two, and this will continue to develop through their teen years. Therefore, it's developmentally appropriate for toddlers to struggle with sharing, since they aren't yet capable of seeing from someone else's perspective. But you can plant the seeds now! You can use books to let your child practice putting themself in someone else's shoes.

Messiness: 1

Activity Time: 20 minutes

MATERIALS:

☐ Picture books

STEPS:

1. Choose (or let your child choose) a picture book to read together. Toddlers love repetition, so this is a great way to add some variety when you're reading the same book for the thousandth time today.

2. If there are illustrations or pictures of people, point out their faces and say what it looks like they're feeling. Ask your child if they would feel that way, too. Try not to ask questions about the plot, but you might want to remind them of what's happening to give them clues to how a character could feel.

3. Ask older toddlers to try and label emotions. Ask them if they would do the same thing in that situation as the character in the book did. Then ask why or why not.

TIP: *Check out your local branch library for book options.*

11. Mirror Faces

Kids love mirrors and funny faces, and you can combine these in an activity to help your toddler build their emotional vocabulary. The sillier and more exaggerated your facial expressions are, the better!

Messiness: 1

Activity Time: 5 minutes

MATERIALS:

☐ Mirror

STEPS:

1. Sit or stand in front of a mirror together and say the name of a feeling. Then make the appropriate facial expression in the mirror.

2. Ask your toddler to make the same face.

3. Try making happy, sad, angry, surprised, and scared faces to start. Then add silly, grumpy, sleepy, etc.

   TIP: *For older toddlers, make a face and ask them to guess what face you're making. Or, ask them to make various faces on their own.*

SKILLS
LEARNED

gross motor
skills

sensory
skills

social
skills

12. Emotional Superheroes

Toddlers are still learning who they are, what they like, and what they can do. Pretending to be someone else allows them to "try on" different personas in a safe environment. Superheroes are larger than life, so their exaggerated actions make a fun basis for big movements and big feelings. This activity is easy to adjust according to your child's interests and abilities as they get older.

Messiness: 2 (if your hero vanquishes many enemies)

Activity Time: 15 minutes

MATERIALS:

☐ Costume items such as a cape (you can use a blanket or towel), hat, gloves, goggles, and belt (optional)

STEPS:

1. Choose a feeling to embody.

2. Name your superhero. Maybe you're Mega Happy Kid, Super Sad Panda, or The World's Grumpiest Giraffe.

3. Identify your superpowers. Do you cheer people up, or do you create situations that cause a certain feeling?

4. Name your nemesis. Who is the "bad guy" in the situation? What's the opposite feeling? How do you destroy it?

   TIP: Use your superhero to create social narrative comics (see page 47).

- 3 -
How My Body Feels

Feelings are how you think about emotions, but emotional responses are physical. When you help kids connect to how their bodies feel during their reactions, they'll have a better understanding of what's happening and how to manage it as they get older. These activities focus on physicality and body awareness with that goal in mind.

13. Belly Butterflies

Kids can get upset stomachs for many reasons, and stress can be a cause. Young kids can't yet separate fantasy from reality, and the unknown can cause them to worry. Helping children identify those feelings allows them to better manage their reactions.

Messiness: 1

Activity Time: 5 minutes

STEPS:

1. If your child's stomach hurts and there doesn't seem to be a physical cause, help them describe how it feels. Does it feel fluttery? Sharp and poky? Like they have a rock in their tummy?

2. Walk them through the process of changing that feeling. Can a deep breath help calm down those butterflies? Can they picture the rock breaking into tiny pieces? What would soothe them?

3. Remind them of what worked last time and that the feeling doesn't last forever.

TIP: *Parents with anxiety are more likely to have kids with anxiety (correlation, not causation). Narrate this process to them when you feel anxious to model how you relieve your anxiety.*

gross motor
skills

sensory
skills

SKILLS
LEARNED

14. Heartbeat Drums

Our hearts beat faster when we're exerting ourselves or when we're under stress. Teaching kids to notice their heartbeats can help them identify anxiety levels when they're older.

Messiness: 2

Preparation Time:
5 minutes

Activity Time: 15 minutes

MATERIALS:

☐ Toy drums or real drums (a plastic container or bucket will work just fine)

☐ Kids who are sensitive to sound may want noise-cancelling headphones (optional)

PREPARATION:

- Set up drums and offer headphones, if desired.

STEPS:

1. Have your child put their hand over their heart and see if they can feel their heartbeat.

2. Tap on the drum to show what a resting heartbeat sounds like. Invite them to play along.

3. Next, explain that when they're excited or scared, their heart beats faster.

4. Try running in place for 20 seconds or doing 10 jumps together. Then have your child put their hand over their heart to feel what their heartbeat is like now.

5. Have them tap out that rhythm with you.

6. Explain that breathing slowly, snuggling, and drinking water can help their heartbeat slow back down to normal.

SKILLS
LEARNED

gross motor
skills

sensory
skills

15. Do I Smell Cookies?

Deep breathing has been shown to reduce stress levels and lower blood pressure. Start this strategy early so kids can cultivate it. If you use deep breaths to calm yourself, let your child know so they see you using the same technique.

Messiness: 1

Activity Time: 5 minutes

STEPS:

1. Ask your child, "What's that smell?" Sniff a bit.

2. Ask again, "Do I smell cookies?" Take a deep, slow breath in through your nose.

3. Next, say, "They're still hot. Let's blow on them to cool them off."

4. Exhale slowly through your mouth.

NOTE: *Unless you decide to use real cookies, it's best to exaggerate these actions so your little one is "in" on the joke of pretend snacks.*

TIP: *Substitute hot chocolate or another favorite food item. Try using a pretend visual aid to help make the action less abstract.*

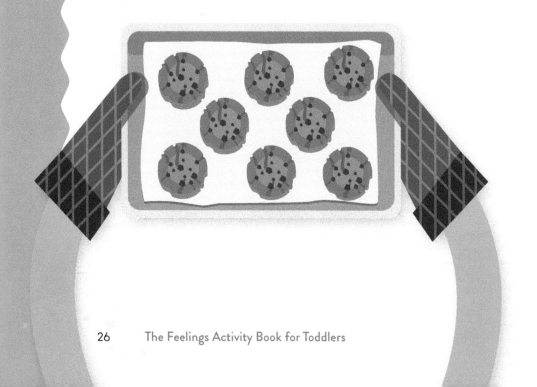

16. Making Pizza

This fun connection game gives your child plenty of sensory input while they help direct the activity. It's meant to be silly and fun, and laughter gives your child a way to release tension and reconnect with you. It also gives your child the chance to practice calming down, since they can't calm down if they're not riled up. Giving them an opportunity during a playful moment helps them feel safe.

Messiness: 1

Activity Time: 10 minutes

STEPS:

1. Get down on the floor with your child and ask if they want to be made into pizza.

2. First make the "dough" by squeezing your child's body into a ball a few times. Then "roll out the dough" by pressing their limbs gently into the floor.

3. Add "sauce" by pretending to pour and smooth it over their body. Ask what toppings they want, or make it silly by offering choices like socks and bananas.

4. Sprinkle "cheese" on the top, slide their body into the "oven," and wait until the timer goes off. Then "slice" the pizza up and gobble a slice down!

   TIP: *Make "sandwiches" using pillows or cushions and gently squishing them in between.*

CAUTION: *If something tickles or your child says "stop," listen to them. It's important for them to have bodily autonomy. Respecting their boundaries teaches kids about consent from an early age.*

SKILLS LEARNED	gross motor skills	receptive communication	sensory skills

17. Lily Pad Float

Our bodies and our brains work together to let us know how we feel. Sometimes when your mind feels calm, your body isn't always relaxed. When your child pretends to be a lily pad, calmly floating on a pond, they can help their mind match their body. Have your child start with a few breaths and try to improve over time.

Messiness: 1

Activity Time: 5 to 10 minutes

MATERIALS:

☐ Pillow

☐ Blanket or yoga mat

STEPS:

1. Have your child lay down on a yoga mat, blanket, floor, or bed.

2. Ask them to close their eyes and imagine a beautiful pond. Have them pretend as though they're a lily pad, floating calmly on the surface.

3. Tell them to breathe in and out to relax their body. Count how many breaths they can take before they have to move.

18. Cotton Ball Races

This can be done as a "race" or a solo activity. If you're "racing" against your child, it can help if you're silly about it and fail dramatically. Using a straw to direct their breath helps kids practice controlled breathing, and seeing the impact on the cotton ball lets them visualize how hard they're breathing. This experience can translate into taking deep breaths when they're upset. The chance to get excited also gives them the opportunity to calm back down again when they're happy.

Messiness: 2

Preparation Time:
5 minutes

Activity Time: 10 minutes

MATERIAL:

☐ Painter's tape or masking tape (optional)

☐ Books or blocks (optional)

☐ Drinking straw (any material)

☐ Cotton ball, craft pom-pom, or a feather

PREPARATION:

▸ If desired, tape a "track" down the length of a table. (This step may make the activity too challenging for younger toddlers.)

▸ To make it easier, stack books or blocks (if using) along the sides like bumpers to keep the cotton ball on the track (think bumper bowling).

STEPS:

1. Place a cotton ball at one end of a table. A kids' table works well for this since it's closer to the ground. You can also do this on non-carpeted floors and have your child lay on their belly.

2. When you say "go," have your child point the straw at the cotton ball and blow through it to move the cotton ball to the other end of the table.

3. Feel free to just let them explore the game without any rules, or encourage them to blow gently so it's easier to direct the cotton ball.

4. Join them for a "race" with two cotton balls side-by-side.

19. Silly and Strong

Toddlers seem so much older and bigger than babies, but they're still brand-new to the planet. They're constantly learning what their bodies can and can't do yet. This activity lets them be silly and feel strong.

Messiness: 1

Activity Time: 10 minutes

MATERIAL:

☐ Yoga mat (optional)

STEPS:

1. Model all these movements next to your child to help them follow along. Stand with your feet about shoulder-width apart. Put your arms up and reach for the sky like a tall, tall mountain.

2. Next, sit down, put the bottoms of your feet together, and pull them toward your body so your knees bend out like butterfly wings. Gently "flap" your knees like a butterfly in the breeze.

3. Roll onto your belly with your legs out behind you. Press your hands under your shoulders to sway your body like a slithering snake.

4. Then get on your hands and knees and wag your tail like a happy puppy.

5. Repeat if desired.

   TIP: *Don't do any activities if they hurt. Listen to your body.*

20. Excitement Explosion

When we don't express our feelings, they get stored inside until we can't hold them in anymore. Without a healthy outlet, we explode. This activity helps your toddler name their feelings and increase body awareness.

Messiness: 1

Activity Time: 5 minutes

STEPS:

1. Have your little one crouch down in a ball.

2. Think of situations that would illicit a strong response to make them excited or upset. For example, they're going to a birthday party, a toy broke, or a family member is coming to visit.

3. For each situation, have them "fill up" with feelings until they can't hold it in anymore and they "pop" like popcorn or fireworks!

4. For older toddlers, try mixing in calming situations that make them stay put or get smaller again.

   TIP: *For a fun visual and snack, make popcorn at home. It's easiest to see if you have an air popper, but the microwave or stove will work, too.*

21. Counting Kangaroos

When kids are bouncing off the walls, often they need a way to channel their energy. This activity works well when you're trying to leave the park or get them into another room.

Messiness: 1

Activity Time: 5 minutes

STEPS:

1. Choose a starting point. This could be marked on the floor somehow, or just starting from where your toddler is standing.

2. Choose an end point. It could be a piece of furniture, a crack in the sidewalk, a doorway, or the car.

3. Ask your little one to hop like a kangaroo (feet together) from the start to the end point in 4 to 10 hops. If they can't hop with both feet yet, they can just take steps, or do their best.

    TIP: *Mix up the travel methods: big or small steps, skip, hop, leap, crawl, etc.*

    CAUTION: *If you're outside near a street or in a parking lot, make sure you're holding hands.*

22. Sifting Sand

Like sorting objects, pouring and sifting are other regulating activities that help calm the nervous system. This activity keeps hands and brains busy while emotions are soothed.

Messiness: potential for 4 (beware of dumpers)

Preparation Time: 10 minutes (the first time only)

Activity Time: 20 minutes

MATERIALS:

- ☐ A plastic bin the size of a shoebox or larger, with a lid
- ☐ Play sand (or kinetic sand, which is less messy but doesn't sift as well)
- ☐ Shells or small animal toys
- ☐ Scoop or measuring cup
- ☐ A small sieve or slotted spoon

PREPARATION:

▸ Place a layer of sand in the bottom of the bin. Add the shells or toys, then add sand until the shells or toys are covered.

STEPS:

1. Put the scoop and sieve in the sand and have your little one scoop and sift for as long as they're interested.

2. When they're done, sweep up any spills, put the lid on the bin, and store it for another day.

   TIP: *Place a towel or mat under the bin to catch any spilled sand. This isn't a great activity for kids who put everything in their mouths or kids who dump everything out.*

CAUTION: *Small objects such as shells can be a choking hazard, so use larger ones and supervise your child while they play.*

SKILLS
LEARNED

cognitive
skills

fine motor
skills

sensory
skills

23. Sorting Beads or Buttons

Toddlers love labeling and categorizing things as they make new connections, discover new things, and make sense out of the world. Putting similar things together is very regulating for the brain, as is this activity.

Messiness: 3

Preparation Time:
5 minutes

Activity Time: 15 minutes

MATERIALS:

☐ Towel (optional)

☐ Mixed large-size beads, buttons, or colored craft pom-poms (you can buy a large container of multicolored pony beads at a craft store)

☐ Muffin tin or small paint palette

☐ A small container or scoop

PREPARATION:

▸ Find a place on the floor or at a table. If the surface is hard, you may want to put down a towel to minimize beads rolling away.

▸ You or your child can scoop a handful of beads into one area of the towel.

STEPS:

1. Invite your child to sort the beads into the muffin tin by color. Younger kids will need more help.

2. If your child tends to dump toys, you may only want to give them a few beads at a time.

TIP: *If your child puts small items in their mouth, wait to do this activity until they are no longer mouthing. Large craft pom-poms are a great alternative for younger children or those who struggle with fine motor skills.*

CAUTION: *Small items can be a choking hazard, so use large craft pom-poms for younger kids and supervise this activity closely.*

24. Magazine Collage Faces

These creative collages use magazine photos so kids can create their own funny faces. The mix-and-match feel helps them notice how different features change facial expressions.

Messiness: 3

Preparation Time: 10 minutes

Activity Time: 20 minutes

MATERIALS:

☐ Magazines or catalogs

☐ Scissors

☐ Glue stick

☐ Paper

PREPARATION:

▸ Collect some magazines and cut out a variety of facial features: eyes, eyebrows, noses, mouths, and ears.

STEPS:

1. Let your child choose from the cutouts and arrange them into a face on the sheet of paper. You can draw an oval on the paper as a guide if they want.

2. Help them glue down the magazine clippings.

3. Ask your child to tell you about the face. How might that person feel, and why?

TIP: *Older toddlers might enjoy drawing a body below the face. It's about the process, not the product, so let them channel their inner Picasso.*

SKILLS
LEARNED

gross motor
skills

sensory
skills

25. Obstacle Course, aka Toddler Ninja Warrior Training

Your instinct may be to prevent your child from taking risks, but risk-taking is an important part of the learning process. Building an obstacle course gives toddlers a way to channel their energy, push themselves physically, and perform a sequence of steps.

Messiness: 4

Preparation Time:
5 minutes, but part of the activity

Activity Time: 15 minutes

MATERIALS:

☐ A chair or small table

☐ A piece of masking tape, rope, jump rope, or string (3 to 6 feet long)

☐ A ball or beanbag

☐ A laundry basket, box, or bucket

☐ Pillows, cushions, or a beanbag chair

PREPARATION:

▸ Collect your materials.

▸ Clear an area of space on the floor.

STEPS:

1. Have your child help you set up for some great heavy work that will assist them in regulating their body.

2. Center the chair or table at one end of the course.

3. Lay the tape or rope down next, lengthwise.

4. Place the ball at the end of the rope, then the basket at a reasonable tossing distance.

5. Leave a few feet of space, then create a nice soft crash pad.

6. Have your child climb under (or over) the chair or table, use the rope as a "balance beam" (or hop over it), stop to toss the ball into the basket, then hop three times before leaping into the crash pad.

7. Repeat as needed. Have them help clean up the obstacle course as part of the activity.

TIP: *This is just one setup that can be altered for different ages and abilities. Have them roll across a blanket or empty space, hop on one foot, crawl through a play tunnel, roll a ball into a box, use a scooter board or ride-on toy, etc. You can use painter's tape to mark a course on the floor.*

CAUTION: *Letting kids push themselves is important, but make sure that everything they're climbing on or under is secure.*

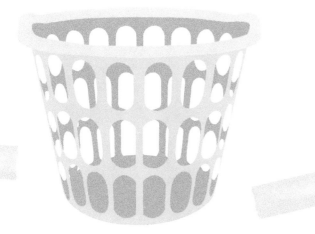

- 4 -
Feelings about Others

Around two to three years old is when toddlers start to understand that other people have their own unique thoughts, ideas, and feelings. This capacity for empathy will continue to develop into their teenage years. These early stages need a lot of support around noticing and understanding social situations and how to manage feelings about other people.

SKILLS
LEARNED

gross motor
skills

sensory
skills

social
skills

26. Super Smash

Anger isn't "bad," it just needs to be expressed without hurting other people. Give kids an outlet to release that tension, like in this activity. If you're worried this will encourage your child to hit, don't be! It actually gives them an opportunity to get that feeling out of their systems safely.

Messiness: 1

Activity Time: 5 minutes

MATERIALS:

☐ A pillow, cushion, or large stuffed animal

STEPS:

1. At a time when your child is relatively calm, ask them to show you how their body feels when they are angry or upset. You can lead them through this and ask questions like:

   a. What does an angry face look like?

   b. Are your fists tight or loose?

   c. Is your mouth smiling or frowning?

   d. Does your body feel hot, cold, or something else?

   e. Are your muscles being squeezed hard or staying soft and relaxed?

2. Then encourage them to take out that anger by punching, hitting, kicking, or jumping on a pillow, cushion, or large stuffed animal. It may sound counterintuitive to tell them to be aggressive, but the goal is to direct the aggression at objects, not people. A typical reaction to this type of aggression is usually negative, so they may need some encouragement if it's something that has been discouraged in the past.

3. Remind them that it's okay to feel angry, and it's okay to jump on and hit pillows, but it's not okay to hit people.

4. The next time they are angry, you can tell them that you notice their fists are clenched and they're frowning, so they look angry. Then you can direct them to the pillow or cushion to let them vent that anger.

5. It's very common for toddlers to hit or kick their parents to release emotional tension. Try to stay calm, block their arm or leg, and simply say, "I won't let you hit me. I see that you're upset, and you can hit this pillow, but not me."

CAUTION: *Make sure to place the pillow or cushion away from tables, chairs, or other obstacles.*

27. The Feelings Detective

It's hard enough to figure out how *you* feel, but then you also have to notice how *other* people feel, too. This activity helps your child notice the signs of emotions in others to improve empathy and social awareness.

Messiness: 1

Activity Time: 10 minutes

MATERIALS:

☐ Books, magazines, or photos with people's faces

STEPS:

1. Find a picture or drawing of a person's face and/or body and show it to your child.

2. Show the picture to your child and point to the eyebrows, eyes, and mouth. Ask them what they think it shows about how that person might feel.

3. If you can see the person's body, ask your child what they notice. For example, are their hands clenched in fists, or relaxed?

4. Put the clues together to figure out how that person is feeling. Then pick a new photo together and try again!

28. Daily Check-In

It's great to talk to your kids about feelings, but it's most important to model how to manage your own. When you talk openly about how you feel, it gives them permission to do the same.

Messiness: 1

Activity Time: 5 minutes

STEPS:

1. During a calm moment, such as mealtime or while getting ready for bed, ask your child how they felt today. They may need a few options from you to choose from.

2. Share how you felt today, too. You may need to go first until your child has tried it a few times.

TIP: *This can be done around the same time each day, such as at dinner, bath time, or bedtime.*

SKILLS
LEARNED

fine motor
skills

receptive
communication

social
skills

29. Taking Turns

Toddlers aren't yet capable of true empathy or sharing, but their brains are working toward it. Taking turns is more concrete than the idea of sharing, and this is an easy way to practice the social cues of whose turn it is.

Messiness: 2

Activity Time: 10 minutes

MATERIALS:

☐ A ball to roll such as a tennis ball or soft inflatable ball

☐ Some open floor space or flat ground

☐ At least 2 people

STEPS:

1. Have your child roll or toss the ball to you and say, "Your turn."

2. You roll or toss the ball to your child (or the next person) and say, "Your turn."

3. Continue taking turns and saying whose turn it is. To mix it up and make them laugh, occasionally pretend to roll the ball, then stop.

TIP: *Younger children may need to use third person (their name, Mom, etc.) since pronouns can be confusing. Nonspeaking kids can point or sign.*

30. Cutout Hearts

Hearts aren't just for Valentine's Day! If you need a simple craft project, add a dash of social-emotional learning when you talk about the reasons why you love your friends and family.

Messiness: 3

Activity Time: 20 minutes

MATERIALS:

☐ Construction paper or cardstock

☐ Scissors

☐ Crayons or markers

STEPS:

1. Trace and cut out heart shapes from the paper.

2. Ask your child to help you think of the names of people who love and care for them. Try using photos for a nonspeaking child.

3. Write each person's name on a heart. On the back, write something your child likes or loves about them.

4. Save the hearts to periodically read to your child as reminders of who loves them, or give (or mail) the hearts to people.

SKILLS
LEARNED

fine motor
skills

social
skills

31. Construction Crew

Building a block tower is a great opportunity to practice taking turns, thinking ahead, and letting kids experience frustration so they are more prepared to manage social situations. If the crashing is too loud or your child seems anxious, you can take turns placing blocks to make a path on the floor that won't fall.

Messiness: 2

Activity Time: 10 minutes

MATERIALS:

☐ Stackable blocks

☐ A clear spot on the floor or a small table

STEPS:

1. Have your child place a block on the floor or table.

2. Take turns placing each block, saying whose turn it is. Count how many blocks tall the tower gets.

3. Try to make it as tall as possible or make a goal and work together to reach a certain height.

   TIP: *If your child tends to throw things, use lightweight or soft blocks.*

32. Social Narratives

Create simple illustrated stories that show, step-by-step, how to navigate new situations. Think of it like an illustrated manual on life for new humans.

Messiness: 2

Activity Time: 20 minutes

MATERIALS:

☐ Paper

☐ Pen or pencil

☐ Stapler, crayons, or markers (optional)

STEPS:

1. Choose an upcoming social situation you want to prepare your child for—for example, going to the dentist or attending a birthday party.

2. Break it down into a few smaller steps.

   a. We will drive to the dentist's office, then we will park the car and go inside.

   b. Next, we will check in at the desk and I may have to write down some information for them.

   c. We will wait in the waiting room for a few minutes, then someone will call your name.

   d. Then we will go to another room and sit in a special chair where you lie down.

   e. The dentist's helper will put a special bib on you to clean your teeth, and then the dentist will look at your teeth to make sure they're okay. They might even take pictures of your teeth.

3. Make squares like a comic strip or format this like a book and put each step on a separate page. Draw each step so your child knows what to expect. It can be easy to skip steps that adults think are obvious, but they aren't actually obvious to kids who haven't had this experience before.

4. Read through this social narrative together in advance of the activity so your child knows what will happen and how to navigate the situation.

SKILLS
LEARNED
gross motor
skills

sensory
skills

33. Blow Me Down!

Toddlers often experience the conflicting feelings of wanting more power and control yet needing to feel safe and secure. Giving them opportunities to feel strong when they can't hurt others helps them practice controlling their strength.

Messiness: 1

Activity Time: 10 minutes

STEPS:

1. Find an open floor space or relatively soft ground.

2. Tell your child, "I bet you can't blow me over!"

3. When they blow a puff of air at you, fall down dramatically, exclaim at how strong they are, and say you didn't think they could do it. Dare them to do it again, get back up, and repeat.

   TIP: *Start from a sitting position to make it easier for you. Standing up makes it more dramatic for your child but is more physically challenging.*

34. The Magic Wand

When you let your child direct an activity, it gives them an opportunity to make choices, be in charge, and navigate interpersonal communication. Adding a magic wand just makes it more fun.

Messiness: 2 (depending on your play director)

Preparation Time: 5 minutes

Activity Time: 15 minutes

MATERIALS:

☐ Wand or a stick, chopstick, drumstick, etc.

☐ Stuffed animals or dolls

PREPARATION:

▸ Collect your materials.

STEPS:

1. Give your child their "wand" and tell them that it's magic. If they use the wand, they can tell their stuffed animals what to do.

2. If there is an upcoming event, like a doctor's appointment or travel plans, you can start with that scenario. You or the stuffed animal can explain your worries about a pretend or future situation, and your child can use the magic wand to solve the problem. It helps them hear those fears out loud, and lets them feel in control of a solution, even if it's pretend.

3. Even if your child suggests silly or violent actions, it's actually helpful for them to work those out through fantasy play. If they have a violent solution, try to transform it. For example, if they say they're shooting you, exclaim that it's a love gun and they're covering you in kisses.

TIP: *Make a wand at home for a fun craft project.*

outdoor activity

35. Chalk It Up

If you ask parents what values they want their children to have, many would say "kindness." Toddlers are limited in the ways they can help others, but this is a fun way to add some kind vibes to an activity.

Messiness: 4

Activity Time: 20 minutes

MATERIAL:

☐ Sidewalk chalk

STEPS:

1. Find a safe area of pavement, sidewalk, or driveway where you're allowed to be. If you know your neighbors, this is a fun way to leave them a friendly message.

2. Model drawing hearts, rainbows, suns, flowers, and other cheerful pictures for your child to encourage them to draw and color. Write positive messages like "You are loved," and read them aloud. Ask them how other people will feel when they see colorful pictures and kind words.

CAUTION: *Get permission before drawing on someone else's sidewalk or driveway.*

36. Memory Jar

Time is too abstract a concept for toddlers, but writing down happy memories lets you revisit the recent past together. You can talk about why a memory is happy when you write it down, then again when you look at the memories later. Having specific situations where they felt a certain way can help kids make sense of their world.

Messiness: 2

Activity Time: 10 minutes

MATERIALS:

☐ Washi tape (optional)

☐ Clear jar, preferably with a lid

☐ Writing utensil

☐ Scraps of paper

STEPS:

1. If desired, use washi tape to make a label for your jar, and tape it on.

2. When you have a funny quotation or anecdote, a positive experience, or a fun event, write it down on a scrap of paper and have your child add it to the jar.

3. Every month, at the end of the year, or just occasionally, revisit the memories in the jar with your child.

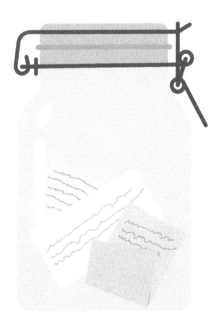

37. Highs and Lows

It can be tempting to cheerlead for your child, but always being positive can invalidate their feelings. When kids are struggling, it's more helpful to acknowledge their challenges. However, you can always draw attention to their strengths.

Messiness: 1

Activity Time: 5 minutes

STEPS:

1. Ask your child something that was challenging or hard today. If they say they don't know, it can help to remind them of what they did earlier in the day. When they do tell you something that was hard for them, you may want to disagree with them ("No, you did great!") but it's best to just listen and validate their feelings ("That was tough for you.").

2. Ask your child about something that made them happy or that went well for them today. You could also phrase it as something they enjoyed, something that made them smile or laugh, or the best part of the day.

3. If they're not speaking much, you may need to lead them through this. You can review the day's activities and have them indicate what they enjoyed or didn't, or they could make a face to show how they felt about it. You could also use visual aids like drawing the choices and have them point to choose.

4. Try to repeat back and paraphrase what they said. For nonspeaking kids, they can confirm what you say. ("So your favorite part of the day was going to the park? Yes? And the hardest part was when we had to leave? That was tough; you wanted to stay and use the swings for a long time.")

TIP: *You can combine this activity with Thumbs-Up/ Thumbs-Down on page 8 or Draw Your Day on page 12 to add gestures and visual elements. This can be especially helpful for nonspeaking kids.*

SKILLS
LEARNED

expressive
communication

sensory
skills

social
skills

38. Box of Hugs

So much of managing feelings and their subsequent behaviors is preventing them from piling up in the first place. Some big feelings are unavoidable and just need to be worked through, but smaller ones can often be diffused throughout the day. This quick connection game provides an easy opportunity to laugh together, plus hugging releases oxytocin, "the love hormone," and makes you both feel good.

Messiness: 1

Activity Time: 5 minutes

MATERIALS:

☐ Box (optional)

STEPS:

1. Ask your child if you can have a hug.

2. Then ask how many hugs they want, because you have a box of hugs and need to know how many to get out. Let them answer or suggest some numbers so they can choose.

3. Either pretend to get a box or use a real one, and mime getting something out of the box. Count the number of squeezes as you hug your child.

4. Ask if they want to get some hugs out of the box, too, and if so, how many?

    TIP: *Bodily autonomy is key, so honor their refusal. You can also suggest they hug a favorite stuffed animal.*

- 5 -
What to Do When I Have Big Feelings

It's easy to forget that our job as parents isn't to prevent or fix feelings, but just to hold space for them. Adults struggle to stay calm and manage their emotions, too; these activities give kids some strategies to practice that can help them calm down when they're upset.

SKILLS LEARNED | fine motor skills | gross motor skills | sensory skills

39. Blowing Bubbles

It's not usually one single event that causes big feelings. Instead, feelings can build up throughout the day until something seemingly small is too much. Finding ways to calm the nervous system before it becomes unmanageable can help prevent meltdowns. Bubbles are easy to stash in a cupboard and inexpensive to make at home. Blowing bubbles helps kids tune in to their bodies and practice deep breathing.

Messiness: 3 (if your kids always dump out the bubble solution)

Preparation Time: 5 minutes (if making bubble solution at home)

Activity Time: 10 minutes

MATERIALS:

- ☐ 1 cup water
- ☐ 2 tablespoons light corn syrup or glycerin
- ☐ 4 tablespoons dishwashing liquid
- ☐ Pipe cleaners or thin wire
- ☐ Store-bought bubble solution (optional)

PREPARATION:

- ▸ To make the bubble solution, gently mix the water, corn syrup, and dishwashing liquid until combined.
- ▸ Bend the pipe cleaner or wire into a loop with a handle to create a bubble wand.

STEPS:

1. Blow bubbles one at a time for your child and count them.

2. Have them blow bubbles. Let them try on their own, then demonstrate and encourage them to blow slowly.

40. Tape Ball Target Practice

If you've ever been angry enough that you wanted to throw something, you'll understand this activity. Kids develop gross motor skills before fine motor skills, so this large body movement can channel their feelings without hurting anyone.

Messiness: 3

Preparation Time:
5 minutes

Activity Time: 10 minutes

MATERIALS:

☐ Light-colored or kraft paper

☐ Black and/or red marker

☐ Packing or masking tape

☐ Newsprint or old magazines

PREPARATION:

▸ Draw a bullseye on the light-colored paper to make a target. Tape it to a wall at a point a little higher than your child's head.

▸ Give your little one a newspaper or magazine. Have them tear out a page and crumple it into a ball that's small enough for your child to hold with one hand. Wrap it loosely with tape to hold the crumpled paper into a ball. You may want to make a few so you don't have to chase them down as often.

STEPS:

1. Practice this first when your child is calm so they're not learning something new when they're upset.

2. If you need a phase for when they are upset, try "It's okay to be mad, but I can't let you hurt anyone. You can throw this instead."

3. Give them the tape ball and have them throw it at the target.

   TIP: *If they prefer it, you can use a bucket or basket as a target. If they get frustrated because it's too hard to aim, just have them throw the ball as far as they can.*

SKILLS
LEARNED

sensory
skills

social
skills

41. Calm Like the Ocean

Emotions are physiological, so the intense physical reactions can make kids even more upset when their bodies feel dysregulated and out of control. Regulating the nervous system can help kids calm their bodies down and help them manage their feelings more effectively. The ocean bottle in this activity gives kids a visual focus to reduce other stimuli, and the movement is soothing to watch.

Messiness: 4

Preparation Time:
10 minutes

Activity Time: 10 minutes

MATERIALS:

☐ Clear bottle with a screw-top lid

☐ Water

☐ Blue food coloring

☐ Vegetable oil

☐ Tape or glue

PREPARATION:

▷ Fill the bottle halfway with water. Add a few drops of food coloring. Carefully fill the rest of the bottle with the oil. Glue the lid on, and/or screw the lid on and tape around it to prevent removal.

STEPS:

1. Ways to use the ocean bottle include: shake it quickly to watch the oil and water separate into bubbles, watch the beads rejoin one another, gently tip it to see the water move, spin or roll the bottle on its side to see what happens, etc.

2. This is a great activity to include in a calming corner or Cozy Kit (page 66). A calming corner is a comfortable, safe space where kids can go when they're upset and having a hard time to use tools and strategies to calm down.

   TIP: *Reuse an 8-ounce plastic water bottle to make a mini version that's great for the car or while waiting in line.*

42. Butterfly Wings

Since emotions are physiological responses to stimuli, physical input can affect how you feel. This simple technique helps calm the body from the outside, and your child can do this on their own.

Messiness: 1

Activity Time: 5 minutes

STEPS:

1. Have your child cross their hands across their chest, palms toward the center of their body. You can help them interlink their thumbs to form "butterfly wings" with their fingertips just below their collarbone.

2. Have them close their eyes, breathe slowly if possible, and "flap" one hand at a time to gently pat their chest, alternating sides.

3. Help them count so they pat each side 6 to 8 times to mimic the wings of a butterfly.

SKILLS
LEARNED

cognitive
skills

fine motor
skills

43. Clothespin Worry Dolls

Worry dolls are a Mayan tradition from what is now Guatemala. According to the traditional story, a child can tell all their worries to a worry doll before going to bed and by morning they wake up with the wisdom of how to make worries disappear. Here's an activity to make a doll inspired by this Mayan legend.

Messiness: 4

Activity Time: 20 minutes

MATERIALS:

- ☐ Yarn or embroidery floss

- ☐ Wooden clothespins, or you can use twigs or wooden craft sticks

- ☐ Craft glue or low-temp hot glue gun and hot glue

- ☐ Craft paint and small paintbrush and/or permanent marker

STEPS:

1. Have your child choose what color "clothes" their doll should have from your yarn/floss options. About ½ inch from the top of the doll, start wrapping the clothespin with yarn to make the doll's clothes. Kids with more developed fine motor skills could help with this step. Use one color or get creative and use many. When you're done wrapping, carefully glue down the end so it doesn't unravel.

2. Ask your child if the doll should have hair, and if so, what color. Use the yarn to make hair. If you cut the pieces and add the glue, your child could add the yarn themself.

3. Use a small paintbrush or the permanent marker to make eyes and a mouth. Your child could do this step if they're able. Let dry if needed.

4. Show your child how they can whisper their worries to their doll. The worry doll can give advice, just listen, or take the worries on for someone.

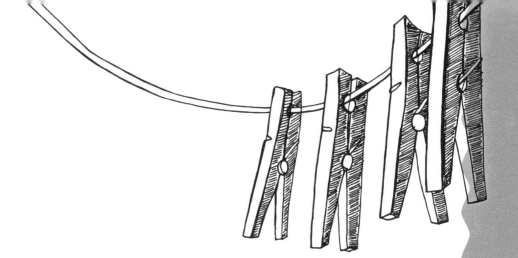

5. Put the worry doll in an accessible place, or the doll can rest under your child's pillow to help them sleep.

   TIP: *If you don't have yarn or glue, you can paint on the clothes instead.*

CAUTION: *If using hot glue, watch the cord and unplug the glue gun immediately.*

SKILLS
LEARNED

cognitive
skills

receptive
communication

44. If Only . . .

Young kids struggle to tell fantasy from reality, which can lead to some big disappointments. This game helps adults practice "wish fulfillment" to help empathize with children. Explaining to kids why they can't have something usually makes them more upset. When you describe what they *do* want, they know you understand and feel heard. Your goal is to have your child saying "yes" to you instead of "no." It may sound like you're agreeing to what they want, but by moving into fantasy territory, it becomes a connection game. Practicing ahead of time gives you experience for when you're trying to empathize under pressure.

Messiness: 1

Activity Time: 10 minutes

STEPS:

1. Try this when your child is calm so you're ready when you need it. It's easier when the stakes are low, like they want to read another book or have another snack (not when they're actually hungry).

2. When your child asks for something they can't have, instead of saying no, reply with the most hyperbolic, extreme version of what they want. For example:

   a. Ice cream? If only we could eat ice cream all day long!

   b. You want that toy? All the toys? If only we could get a million toys!

   c. You don't want to leave. If only we could stay at the park forever and ever!

3. Next, follow it up with questions so they're involved. Using the same examples:

   a. What flavor would you eat first? How many flavors can you think of?

   b. Do you think a hundred toy trucks would fit in our house? How about a million?

   c. If we stay forever, where are you going to sleep? On a swing? On the slide? In a tree?

4. Keep suggesting silly solutions connected to their request. You will know it worked when they're laughing, or they're telling *you* "no."

SKILLS
LEARNED
cognitive
skills

sensory
skills

45. Cozy Kit

Calming strategies don't work if you can't think of them when you're stressed. Putting together a "cozy kit" helps kids think through what might help and creates a resource that's ready to use when they need it.

Messiness: 2

Activity Time: 15 minutes

MATERIALS:

- ☐ Box, basket, or other container to put items in
- ☐ Blanket or stuffed animal
- ☐ Favorite book
- ☐ Calming glitter bottle or Calm Like the Ocean bottle (page 60)
- ☐ Any other toy or activity that is calming or regulating

STEPS:

1. Collect all the items and have your little one help you put them in your chosen container.

2. Have your child help decide where to keep the Cozy Kit. A low-traffic area near a comfortable chair, in a corner, or in a play tent are a few options.

3. When your child is upset, ask if they would like their Cozy Kit. Let them choose a soothing item to help them calm down.

gross motor
skills

sensory
skills

SKILLS
LEARNED

46. Play Dough Pancakes

Squishing and squeezing play dough engages a lot of muscles that can help calm the body down. Dough is safe to hit and pinch and gives kids a creative outlet. Not bad for a ball of mush!

Messiness: 3

Activity Time: 15 minutes

MATERIALS:

☐ Play dough or clay

☐ Flat surface

☐ Tools such as a rolling pin, cookie cutters, a plastic knife, etc. (optional)

STEPS:

1. Let your child explore the play dough and play with it freely. Some suggestions for manipulating the play dough follow; demonstrate if needed.

2. Roll small pieces of dough between both hands to form small balls, then smash them flat with the palm of your hand into "pancakes."

3. Against the flat surface, roll the dough with the palm of your hand in an up and down movement on the table to form a long "snake."

4. Pat the dough flat and use cookie cutters to cut out shapes.

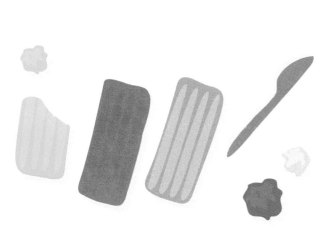

47. Simple Signs

Although many toddlers experience bursts of verbal development, not all do. And even so, when emotions are high, the ability to speak can vanish. Learning some useful words in American Sign Language (ASL) can smooth communication, even for hearing folks.

Messiness: 1

Activity Time: 10 minutes

MATERIALS:

- ☐ American Sign Language (ASL) instructional book or reference guide
- ☐ ASL videos (see the Resources on page 75)

STEPS:

1. Identify situations when your child may struggle to communicate verbally. If they aren't speaking yet (or at all), notice when they seem most frustrated by communication challenges.

2. Make a list of words or phrases that would help, then look them up. Videos are so helpful—just be aware that American, British, and other sign languages are as different from each other as spoken languages are.

3. Practice, practice, practice! Add ASL when you're speaking to reinforce what you're communicating and model its use for your child. Ask questions with two signs as their choices.

4. Don't push your child to sign back before they're ready. Just keep signing and they'll use what they need.

TIP: *ASL is an entire unique language of gestures with its own grammar and cultural rules. If you're trying to tally a new talker's number of words, signs in ASL count! Here are some ideas for first signs to learn: happy, sad, grumpy, sleepy, eat, drink, water, bath, hurt, where, and "I love you." ASL is a beautiful way to communicate, and the alphabet on the next page is a great way to get started.*

48. Blanket Burritos

Firm pressure, like a big hug, is very calming for the nervous system. A simple way for kids to get similar sensory input is by wrapping up snugly in a blanket. Helping your child is an opportunity for connection, and keeping it silly and getting a laugh releases tension and stress so they're better able to manage feelings as they come up. Make sure to follow your child's lead on what feels comfortable and safe for them.

Messiness: 2

Activity Time: 10 minutes

MATERIALS:

☐ Medium-size blanket

☐ Clear floor space

STEPS:

1. Make sure your child is calm and rested for your first attempt of this activity. If they like Blanket Burritos, they can use it later as a strategy when they're upset.

2. Lay out the blanket "tortilla" on the floor. Have your child lie down along one edge with their head off the end of the blanket so it doesn't get wrapped inside. You can describe the various burrito fillings you want to put in your delicious meal.

3. Hold the edge of the blanket to their body and roll your child up inside the blanket. Tell them you're making sure none of the fillings fall out. Make sure their face is clear.

4. Check that they are comfortable. You can leave them on the floor until they want to get out if that's what they want, or you can pick them up and pretend to devour your tasty burrito. If they want more input, you can grab the blanket "tail" near their feet and carefully drag them around.

TIP: *Some people don't like feeling constricted, whereas others love the pressure of being wrapped up. If it's too much, try folding them gently in a blanket "quesadilla" where the blanket only blocks visual input.*

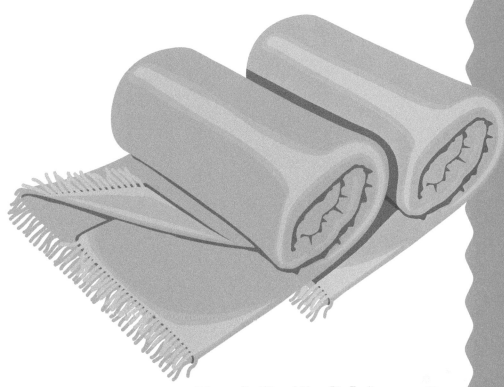

SKILLS
LEARNED

gross motor
skills

sensory
skills

social
skills

49. Rampage!

Let your toddler embrace their inner Godzilla by providing them with opportunities to smash things. Having a safe place to be destructive makes them less likely to test this power on other people.

Messiness: 3

Preparation Time:
5 minutes

Activity Time: 15 minutes

MATERIALS:

☐ Cushions and pillows, or lightweight reusable plastic containers that can stack into a tower

PREPARATION:

▸ Collect your stacking materials in one area.

▸ Clear the area of fragile, breakable, or sharp objects.

STEPS:

1. Ask your child to help you stack up a tower of pillows or containers.

2. When it's tall enough, or it won't stay up anymore, have your child count to three with you.

3. Tell them that at the count of three, they should unleash their best rampaging monster or wrecking ball attack to smash into the tower and knock it over. Repeat.

4. When they've had enough smashing, ask your child to help you put the materials back where they belong.

50. The "No" Game

Toddlers often hear the word "no" more than 40 times per day. No wonder they say it back so often! This game turns it around—the sillier, the better! When you encourage them to refuse you while playing, it's a safe space. They get to feel powerful and in control. That combination of factors is perfect for letting kids process their feelings through play. It may feel like you're giving in by "letting" your child say no, but letting them say no now means they're more likely to cooperate later when you actually need them to!

Messiness: 1

Activity Time: 10 minutes

STEPS:

1. If your child seems like they can only say no, ask them silly questions where "no" is the correct answer.

   - Can I wear shoes on my head?
   - Can I fly to the moon?
   - Can I get a pet alligator?
   - Can I eat all the cheese in the whole world?

2. Try to keep going until they're laughing too hard to say "no." Normal questions will sound much more reasonable to them afterward.

RESOURCES

ASL Resources

American Sign Language for Kids:
***101 Easy Signs for Nonverbal Communication* by Rochelle Barlow**

This book includes a great round-up of signs that can be used for everyday communication for nonverbal children.

Sign Language 101

This website has a variety of free beginner ASL videos as well as paid courses for more in-depth study of both the language and culture.
signlanguage101.com/free-lessons/asl-level-1

Asian Signers is a Deaf-led nonprofit on Instagram (@asiansigners), Facebook (facebook.com/asiansigners), and YouTube (Asian Signers).

Deaf Family Matters is on Instagram (@deaffamilymatters), TikTok (@deaffamilymatters), Facebook (facebook.com/deaffamilymatters), and YouTube (Deaf Family Matters).

What the Deaf?!

Cohosted by two Deaf women, this podcast offers insight into Deaf culture.
whatthedeaf.com

The Ariel Series

A queer, Deaf couple's journey to parenthood and life with their toddler.
thearielseries.com

Books for Parents

Understanding Your Child's Sensory Signals **by Angie Voss**

This book is an incredible resource; it explains certain behaviors that are due to sensory regulation issues and how to help manage them. Kids who need more support regulating their bodies can feel anxious when dysregulated, which makes their feelings especially intense.

Playful Parenting **by Lawrence J. Cohen**

The author is a child psychologist and a dad. He combines his experience to offer suggestions on how play can help you connect with your kids.

When your toddler gets older, try these books for kids ages 4 to 8:

Positive Behavior Activities for Kids by Stacy Spensley

The Feelings Activity Book for Children by Diane Romo

Books for Kids

Happy Hippo, Angry Duck **by Sandra Boynton**

This is a rhyming board book about feelings.

The Way I Feel **by Janan Cain**

This picture book names different feelings.

REFERENCES

Ackerley, Rochelle, Jean-Marc Aimonetti, and Edith Ribot-Ciscar. "Emotions Alter Muscle Proprioceptive Coding of Movements in Humans." *Scientific Reports* 7, no. 8465 (2017). doi.org/10.1038/s41598-017-08721-4.

Artigas, Lucina, Ignacio Nacho Jarero, et al. *EMDR and Traumatic Stress after Natural Disasters: Integrative Treatment Protocol and the Butterfly Hug.* Poster presented at the EMDRIA Conference, Toronto, Ontario, Canada, 2000.

Shafir, Tal. "Using Movement to Regulate Emotion: Neurophysiological Findings and Their Application in Psychotherapy." *Frontiers in Psychology* 7, no. 1451 (September 2016). doi.org/10.3389/fpsyg.2016.01451.

Acknowledgments

Special thanks to my mom for grandma-ing really hard while I wrote this book.

Marissa Anderson is an incredible pediatric occupational therapist, mom, and friend who patiently answers all my random text messages.

About the Author

 Stacy Spensley is a parenting coach, author, podcaster, and tired mama of three children. As the founder of Semi-Crunchy Mama, she provides support and resources for parents so they feel confident in making the best choices for their families. She lives in San Diego with her children, husband, cats, and chickens, and she spends most of her time feeding her children and staying up too late reading. Learn more at semicrunchymama.com or message her on social media.